Ruth Ann – We hope you can read this in your spare time... and maybe to Renee. I found it so sweet and made me appreciate the many blessings God has given us!

BLESSINGS

Love you,

Joanne

November 20, 2009

From the Editors of Good Housekeeping

BLESSINGS

Reflections on Gratitude, Love,
and What Makes Us Happy

HEARST BOOKS
A division of Sterling Publishing Co., Inc.

New York / London
www.sterlingpublishing.com

Contents

Family

Nourishment

Friendship

Introduction

Welcome to *Good Housekeeping's Blessings*. This book grew organically out of one of *Good Housekeeping's* most popular monthly departments, our back-page *Blessings* essays. In the magazine, as in this book, we have invited some of America's most beloved writers to offer personal, poignant, and sometimes funny reminiscences of the people and moments that made a difference in their lives. You may already have favorite *Blessings* writers such as Elizabeth Berg, Maeve Binchy, Alice Hoffman, Jacquelyn Mitchard, and Jodi Picoult. You'll also be moved by other authors in the book, from Lucinda Franks to Chitra Banerjee Divakaruni.

How have *you* been blessed? Perhaps by the child you thought you couldn't have, or a stranger who changed your life in ways she'll never know. Study after study has shown that being aware of the blessings in your life makes you a happier person. I hope our *Blessings* will remind you of what's wonderful and worth celebrating in your life, as it has for me.

Rosemary Ellis
Editor in Chief
Good Housekeeping

Motherhood

God Moves in a
Mysterious Way

BY

*Luanne
Rice*

The holidays in our house were close to magic. In my memory, there was always snow—deep enough to build snowmen and snow forts. My sisters and I would go out to play, and when we came back inside—our cheeks hurting from the cold, mittens frozen with tiny balls of ice—our mother would give us hot chocolate in special Santa mugs. Those mugs would have been pulled out of the cold cellar the first week of December, along with boxes of decorations. The thin cardboard boxes were themselves practically heirlooms: ancient, falling apart, filled with honeycomb inserts to hold and protect our glass Christmas tree ornaments. We knew each one and grieved with a tiny shock when a favorite would drop and break. For the tree-top, we used a starfish—the biggest one we'd ever found—to remind us of happy times at the beach.

My mother taught us to treasure our holiday things, because they were part of our family story. Our family had its share of worries and mysteries. But there was something in the way my mother wove a spell of gingerbread, pine, red ribbons, and candlelight. The trappings and traditions seemed talismanic; I think she intended them, literally, to protect us from life's sorrows and disappointments. An English teacher, she read us Dickens. My sisters and I attended school with girls and boys from the local Children's Home, and imagining my friends—foster children—without their mothers to read to them was almost impossible to bear. My mother didn't sugarcoat the truth, but she told us that we were lucky to have each other, that love was the greatest gift of all.

> Something made me put up a small tree by her bedside, even though she couldn't see it.

After I grew up, no matter where I lived, I returned home for Christmas. One December, my mother became ill with a brain tumor and had to go into a nursing home. The coldness and darkness of the season seemed so real then, so true; I felt as if from then on, the holidays would remind me only of winter, and of her dying.

But God moves in a mysterious way. And so did my mother. All her years of love and hope, red ribbons and pine boughs took hold. Something made me put up a small tree by her bedside, even though she couldn't see it. I

pulled out the old boxes, brought some of her ornaments and the starfish to her room. She'd been in a coma for a week—hadn't opened her eyes in all that time. It was dark, except for the tiny white tree lights. I looked over and saw her staring at me. Her gaze was steady; I had the feeling she was trying to memorize me. Her lips moved. "I love you," she said. "I love you," I said back.

She didn't die that night, but soon afterward. God does move in a mysterious way. He does, He does. The rest of the proverb goes, "His wonders to perform." In spite of what I feared most about losing my mother at that time of year, the holidays have remained a time of joy. They remind me of her spirit, of what she believed about the season: that loving each other is the greatest gift—the greatest wonder—of all. I have her in my heart, and I believe she has me in hers.

People Who Live in Glass Houses Shouldn't Throw Stones

BY
Alice
Hoffman

I learned about glass houses and stones from my mother, although it was years before I realized what exactly she had taught me. She was so unlike the other mothers I knew growing up that I saw her as lacking.

My mother was the only divorced woman in our neighborhood, and the only one with a nine-to-five job. She had neither the time nor the inclination for domestic duties. We spent Thanksgivings at a local French restaurant, where the only other customers were stewardesses from overseas. She was a fool for love. In an era when people simply didn't live together without benefit of marriage, my mother did, and many of my friends were not allowed to come to our house. Their parents had an arsenal of stones.

By the time I was 13, I had a pocketful as well. I resented everything about my mother. It didn't matter that she was smart and beautiful, that she was a great friend, a rebel, that she had more books on her shelves than anyone else in our town. In my eyes, she was a failure as a mother.

It was a time of judgment back then, the early 1960s. Especially for girls who didn't adhere to the rules (unspoken, unwritten, but there all the same). In my high school, girls who became pregnant simply disappeared. For all we knew, the earth might have opened up to swallow them. We never saw them again. But my mother saw them. She was a social worker who worked first with unwed mothers, then in foster care, and then, following the spiral that often occurs, in protective services.

> It was in that car, on that day, that I felt just how heavy the stones in my pocket were.

As a teenager, I sometimes helped her pick up babies and deliver them to foster homes. One day we went to pick up twins; the babies had red hair and were solemn and quiet. The woman at the desk thought I was the mother.

There were no infant seats in those days, and no seatbelts, only plastic laundry baskets softened with quilts. We propped up a laundry basket in the front seat of the car; my mother drove with one arm thrown over the steering wheel and held on to the basket with her free hand. I sat in the back with the second baby.

Going out to the foster home, I almost had the sense that these really were my babies, and I had an even deeper sense of what it must have meant for the mother to give them up. I thought about those girls who had disappeared from my school and the friends who weren't allowed to come to my house. I thought about judgment and stones and the damage that could result. I thought of the girls my mother had helped, of those who went on to have their babies and those who could not go forward with their pregnancies. It was in that car, on that day, that I felt just how heavy the stones in my pocket were.

Lives are complicated, messy, never exactly what we plan. As for glass houses, we all live in one. Eventually, someone is bound to come along and throw stones. But the way you live your life is up to you. This is what I learned from my mother, an admirable woman who wasn't afraid of snide remarks or choices that differed from her own. When stones and rocks are thrown, you can let them get you down or you can turn them into something worthwhile—a shelter for your body or your soul, a wall with which you can surround your garden, a place where anything can grow.

Karma on Credit

BY

Firoozeh
Dumas

My foray into philanthropy began with a play-date. Watching the nanny play with our children, I told my friend how lucky she was to have found such a loving caretaker. "Maria has a 2-year-old son, so she's great with kids," she told me.

"Where is he?" I asked.

"In El Salvador," my friend said. Maria was one of the many women who come to the United States to earn money while their children remain behind, often with grandparents. Maria was hoping to visit her son in a year.

I couldn't go to sleep that night knowing that this woman, who'd been hugging my child, could hug her own child only in her dreams. Even if she went home in a year, she'd have missed 12 months of her child's life. That's an eternity. Would he even recognize her? I decided that instead of having a first-birthday party for my son, which he wouldn't remember anyway, I'd give the money to Maria.

The next day, I went back to my friend's house and handed Maria an envelope. In broken Spanish, I said that I hoped she would see her son soon. Maria looked very confused until I held out my arms like an airplane while saying "El Salvador" and "*niño*" repeatedly. She finally understood and started to cry. I decided that from then on, I'd celebrate my children's birthdays by helping someone else.

> I decided that from then on, I'd celebrate my children's birthdays by helping someone else.

Over the years, we donated clothes for children in Romania and purchased honeybees for poor farmers in Africa. My children got hooked, too. Then I had the brilliant idea of charging our donations to my credit card and earning mileage. My husband and I wanted to take the kids to Paris, and it seemed an easy way to get a little closer to a genuine *pain au chocolat*.

One day, I saw an ad for an essay contest sponsored by my credit card company. The grand prize was 100,000 miles. I wrote about combining karma and my credit card and won first place. "You're always winning things," my relatives said. This is true. I won a two-month trip to Paris in a speech contest when I was 17. (I later married a Frenchman. *Le destin,* as they say.)

Before I could book the flight to Paris, one of my aunts in Iran phoned me. Her son had been laid off and was going through a rough time. Could I give him my miles so he could fly home? With my husband's blessing, we decided our *pain au chocolat* could wait.

A few months later, we received a letter from the IRS reminding us we owed a thousand dollars due to the value of the miles. As my husband wrote the check, grumbling about "not being able to afford winning," the realization struck me: If someone in my family gets sick, he can go to the doctor. We live in a house that is warm in the winter and cool in the summer. I have the "burden" of trying to lose weight because we have access to so much good food. More important, I can hug my children whenever I want. What else is there to win?

Birthday Wishes

BY

*Claire
Cook*

On a Saturday morning in 1966, I knocked at my best friend's front door. "My mother died," I said the second she opened it.

"No, sir," she swore, though since this was a Boston suburb, it sounded more like "No, suh." Today, she'd have said, "No way."

"Swear to gawd," I said. *Way.*

"Liar," she said. "You're making it up."

I wasn't. The day before, my mother's flu had turned into sepsis. She slipped into a coma at the hospital and never came out, leaving five children under the age of 12 motherless. Neighbors met us in our driveway after school and brought us home with them. They didn't say much, but I knew my first pajama party, scheduled for that evening, was definitely canceled.

The funeral took place on Valentine's Day, also my birthday. Back at the house, someone stuck candles on a dull chocolate cake, so unlike the heart-shaped, candy-studded pink ones my mother had baked for my other 10 birthdays, and mourners sang "Happy Birthday" to me. After that, people started tucking bills—mostly ones and fives, and one hundred-dollar bill—into the pocket of my dress, as if I were a stripper-in-training. My mother would have found the whole thing incredibly tacky.

Over the years, I've met other women who lost their mom at an age when she was still the sun and the moon and their favorite hula hoop all rolled into one, yet were also on the cusp of needing her to walk them through that first period or bra. Time heals many wounds but this loss becomes the defining sadness of your life. By the time I came out of my posttraumatic fog and really wanted to know what my mother had been like—as a person, a woman, a friend—the people who could have told me about her were either dead or long gone.

> What surprised me was knowing that a spirit like hers could live on for decades in the heart of a friend.

Then last summer I did a book signing near my mother's hometown of Holyoke, MA. A woman my age waited in line with an older lady in a wheelchair. The younger woman told me her mother had something to say to me. I leaned over the wheelchair and smiled.

"Your mother was the most generous friend in the world. I went into labor with my son, Jimmy, in the middle of a blizzard," she said. A chill ran down my spine. "The snow came on so fast, my husband couldn't get home. I called the ambulance. I called the police. Nobody came. I called your mother. 'Put your coat on,' she said. 'It will be the adventure of a lifetime.'" She giggled. "Your mother walked me all the way to the hospital through the snow, laughing and joking the whole time."

I reached out to hold her cool, dry hand, and it felt lighter than air. "She was Jimmy's godmother, you know. Your mother had more godchildren than you could shake a stick at."

I'd been old enough to know my mother was big-hearted, to remember the pile of cards, with family photos tucked in, at Christmastime. What surprised me, and made me forever grateful, was knowing that a spirit like hers could live on for decades in the heart of a friend.

Special Delivery

BY

Sarah
Bird

Postpartum depression, I was ready for that. But *pre-partum*? From the instant that sperm collided with egg for my first and only pregnancy, I was knocked off balance. The hormonal lunacy was compounded when my three best friends—the ones who'd pledged that if I went ahead and used the last 15 minutes of fertility left on my biological clock, they would see me through—all abruptly moved away.

Friendless and freaked-out, I felt like a pioneer wife alone on the edge of the frontier. Even though I had the world's sweetest, most attentive husband, a deep, primal need took hold. I wanted my mother.

We, all her six children, always had. She'd been a labor-and-delivery nurse, an army nurse, and a school nurse and had finished her career at a women's health center. She loved to laugh and appreciated a good margarita. What pregnant lady wouldn't have wanted Nurse Bird?

But I couldn't have her. She was a long plane ride away and couldn't leave my ailing father. So we ran up enormous phone bills dissecting every varicose vein and Braxton Hicks contraction. As I lumbered toward the mid-August due date, my anxiety climbed along with the temperature. Then, miracle of miracles, my amazing sisters patched together a plan for a few days of care for my father. If our timing was right, it would allow what I wanted most—my mom to be with me for the delivery.

Even though I had the world's sweetest, most attentive husband, I wanted my mother.

We were all on red alert when I went for a checkup, but my doctor said I was at least a week away from D-day. I rushed home to call my mom and tell her to unpack. Instead, a message was waiting for me: She'd had a "feeling" and was on her way.

Heartbroken, my husband and I picked her up at the airport with the news that she was too early. Her visit would be wasted. On the glum ride home, Nurse Bird decided we needed a drink.

We stopped at a café, and while my mom and husband slurped margaritas, I sipped a smoothie. Perfectly in tune with my mood, a rainstorm raged. Then, halfway through

The author, after giving birth, flanked by her husband and mom

my drink, I spasmodically gripped the edge of the table, and Nurse Bird peeked at the watch she'd used to take a thousand pulses. "Mom," I told her, "it's not what you think." She smiled and kept timing.

We walked outside to a sight I had never witnessed in all the years we'd lived in Texas: a rainbow shimmering across an August sky. An hour later, my water broke. My husband was wonderful during the delivery, but it was my mother's hand that I gripped for dear life.

She's been gone almost three years, yet the blessing of her arrival when I needed her most remains—a facet of my greatest blessing, that Nurse Bird was my mother.

Blowing Kisses

BY

*Leah
Hager Cohen*

My mother has never been one to play about with airy signs of affection. She doesn't flirt or dabble at love. If she hugs you, she means it. That must account for my bias against blown kisses, which have always struck me as being rather coy.

My view softened when my 8-year-old daughter began to incorporate one into her bedtime ritual. I don't know what prompted her to make a blown kiss the last thing she does before I leave her room. But, coming from her, I know that it is the real thing. Still, it was another blown kiss that changed my idea of what such a gesture could contain—and it sprang from the unlikeliest pair of lips: my mother's.

It occurred last summer, after her surgery for ovarian cancer. She had just been transferred back to a regular hospital room from intensive care, but was still "in pieces," as she put it semi-coherently. She was so incapacitated, she needed to have her dry mouth moistened for her—

she could not manage to hold the swab and put it to her own mouth.

In the next bed, behind a curtain, lay another woman who was about to be taken to surgery. We'd gathered from the conversation of the family and doctor that her situation was grave, much worse than my mother's. Eventually, a nurse brought her out from behind the curtain and wheeled her past the end of my mother's bed, toward the door. There was a bit of confusion, people clearing a path. I myself was unsure where to look—away, perhaps, to afford her some privacy. My gaze traveled over the patient's head, toward my mother's bed. My mother was looking straight at her. And with her hand that was too weak even to moisten her own mouth, she blew this woman a kiss.

> Just before she disappeared around the corner, the woman raised her own hand and blew a kiss back.

It took my breath away to recognize the depth of love in the gesture, the kinship and strength, and also resistance. Because in the context of the hospital, the tubes and monitors, the statistics and pathologies and prognoses, my mother's kiss seemed an almost rebellious affirmation of humanity. And possibility.

I'm not talking about surviving the surgery, and the cancer (although of course that possibility, however slim for this woman, existed). I'm talking about the possibility—already blooming in that moment—of contact with another human being across a great empty space.

Just before her wheelchair disappeared around the corner, the woman—small, dark, in her 50s—raised her own hand and blew a kiss back. They never exchanged a word, she and my mother—they hadn't even exchanged names—and I do not know whether anyone else in the room caught what had passed between them. But in that moment, I knew my mother to be more brave and passionate than I had even guessed.

Fatherhood

The Day I Became a Daddy

BY

Chris Chesak

My first child was born on December 16, 2004, just before I flew into Iraq with the Army National Guard. Sitting in a tented phone center at an air base in Kuwait, I was on the line as my wife, Sally, gave birth. From half a planet away, I heard my daughter's first tiny cries. One hour later, I boarded a transport plane headed into the war zone.

Deployed so far from my family, I had to forget about home and focus on the mission. I eased Humvees through rain-soaked palm groves and over slick mud roads, shivered in guard towers through freezing winter dawns, and spent 22 hours guarding a polling place during the national elections. After five months, I was granted a two-week leave and flew home to Boise, Idaho, to meet my daughter, Lillian.

The first morning, still jet-lagged, I woke early and went into her room. As I approached the crib, Lillian's eyes locked on mine. She smiled, and my heart melted. Over the next few days, I became enraptured with her staccato laughs, her sweet cooing, and her determined attempts to crawl. But you're never really home while you're on leave.

In what may be the sweetest blessing of my life, the distance that had come between us finally disappeared.

You can't stop thinking about having to go back. The night before my return flight, I stayed up until 4:00 A.M., my stomach in knots. Too soon, I was in the Middle East again.

Now that I knew what I was missing at home, the days in Iraq became interminable. I stood sweating in the gunner's turret of an armored Humvee and wondered if Lillian was sleeping well, held lonely vigil in a concrete guard tower and thought about what she was eating. My only relief came from a Webcam. Each night, on my laptop, I watched Lillian nurse or nap angelically on Sally's lap. From ten time zones away, I watched her grow as car bombs rattled our barracks' windows. Slowly, the countdown to our departure date went from triple digits to double and then, unbelievably, to single days.

When at last my plane landed in Boise, I searched the crowd of families gathered on the tarmac and found my wife. We didn't say a thing, just hugged and kissed for about six minutes straight. Then Sally handed me my 11-month-

With wife Sally
and baby Lillian

old daughter, and I held her in my arms. But Lillian pushed me away. She didn't know who I was.

Still, after 333 days at war, I was home. And slowly, Lilli Bean became comfortable with me. In what may be the sweetest blessing of my life, the distance that had come between us finally disappeared. One day, after I'd been back for a while, my daughter and I danced in the living room. At last, I got to say the words I'd dreamed of saying: "Hello, Lillian Rose Chesak. I love you. Welcome to the world."

What My Father Saw

BY

Lucinda
Franks

The telescope was my mother's idea. My father was away on business trips so often that when he came home, she'd think up ways to bring him together with his children. Her machinations worked. I lived for those clear nights, just he and I in the middle of the dew-soaked lawn, peering cheek to cheek through the lens. My mother would stand at the window, a wistful little smile on her face.

But as I grew into adolescence, my father and I hurtled out of each other's orbit. He became emotionally absent, light-years away from the Daddy I worshipped. Eventually, my mother died, and my father and I continued to live under different skies. The tension eased after I married, but being with him was still a strain: We couldn't think of anything to talk about.

Then one day, on a whim, I bought a portable red telescope and watched as he and my youngest child, age 6, gravitated toward it. "Look, Amy," Dad said, adjusting the lens. "There's the North Star." Soon, he was putting his arm around her and pointing to a curve of stars as they took shape in the darkening sky. "It's the Big Dipper!" she cried out triumphantly. I felt a twinge of bittersweet joy seeing how Amy's very presence could light up his dour but still handsome face. For her sake, I left the red telescope at his house, and whenever we arrived I'd carefully polish the lens and put it outside, ready for their stargazing.

> I forgave my father. In fact, I fell in love with him all over again.

By then my aging father was spending his days in a bathrobe so full of holes, it looked as if it had been sprayed with a machine gun. One day, I heard Amy's voice saying, "Grandpop, let's put on some clothes. Come with me." I saw her tugging at his hand, leading him into the bedroom. He emerged fully dressed, complete with socks and shoes. "See Mom," whispered my daughter with sly pride. "When you scream for somebody to do something, that makes them not want to do it even more."

Not long after, I found a shoebox filled with his wartime letters to my mother. I opened a packet marked *1943-45* and read with astonishment. The letters were full of so much exuberance and passion for life, I checked the signature to be sure it was my father's. And then, in a packet marked *summer, 1945,* I found the tone had changed to one now familiar to me: distant, dry, devoid of emotion. Something had happened to him.

I prodded Dad for details, handling him as gently as my daughter had, until finally he divulged what he'd been ordered to do. I listened, rapt, as he described the enemy soldiers he'd killed and could never forget, and the survivors of the concentration camp he'd liberated, who still haunted him. The silence I'd taken for hostility was in fact stoicism. He had tried to protect us. I forgave my father. In fact, I fell in love with him all over again.

"Come with us," said Amy one night as they bundled up to track the stars. She'd been secretly listening to our talks. The lens of the red telescope was wider than the one I had known years before. There was room for all three of us to peer up at Orion lifting his lance, his brilliant belt flashing diamonds in the sky.

Don't Make a Mountain out of a Molehill

Betsy Carter

Bras were a big deal in seventh grade. Boys would run their fingers down your back to see if they could catch the strips of elastic band. Sometimes, they'd pull them and the elastic would make a snapping sound. All the cool girls wore bras.

About a month into seventh grade, after much cajoling, I convinced my mother to buy me a training bra. The concept strikes me as funny now. Was it a bra with little wheels? Was it a bra studying to be a bra? But at the time, there was nothing funny about it. My mother took me to Jordan Marsh, our local department store, and she and the saleslady never exchanged knowing looks nor cracked a smile. I tried on many trainees, but the one I finally chose had stitching on the cups in the pattern of brickwork. It was a size 28AAA and was flatter than a pot holder.

That night, after we got home, I overheard my mother tell my father what we'd done. "What does she need a brassiere for?" he asked. "Isn't she making a mountain out of a molehill?"

I thought I would die from embarrassment, I had grudges against my father, and this was one I would certainly add to the list. He was sarcastic and had a blistering temper.

> He sat by my bed, and for the first time in my life, I saw him cry.

I had a big mouth and knew exactly how to provoke him. The air was uneasy between us.

One of my biggest grudges was that my parents were immigrants and never managed to lose their accents. Whenever they could, they'd pop off an Americanism with great pride. When they had friends over, and my mother would serve a big pot roast or one of her famous yeast cakes, someone would inevitably sigh: "Ah, you outdid yourself. This is too much." My father would always shoot back: "Eat what you can, and what you can't we'll can"—and each time he would laugh as if he'd never said it before. When you are 12, being different in any way is unbearable. I rarely invited friends home.

I kept the bra in my bedroom drawer, wrapped in the white tissue from Jordan Marsh. Each morning, I'd take it out of the drawer, unwrap it, wear it to school, and the moment I came home, I'd take it off, wrap it back up in the paper, put it in the drawer, slip into my shorts and T-shirt, and go outside and ride my bike. No one ever tried to snap my band.

The author at 12

My mother died ten years ago. By necessity, my father and I had to deal with each other on different terms. He'd cared for my mother ferociously during her illness, and I saw a strength in him I hadn't recognized before. During this time, I had a mastectomy, and he came to visit me. He sat by my bed, and for the first time in my life, I saw him cry. "You were always such a sunny child," he said, in an unusual show of emotion. "I can't stand to see you in pain."

Later, when he was pushing 90 and taking yoga classes and learning how to swim, his spirit and resilience stunned me. "Dad, you're really doing great," I said, paying him a rare compliment.

"I'm doing the best I can," he said.

"And what you can't you'll can?" I asked.

By then, I'd called a truce. The air was softer between us, and I realized that he'd taught me something about grudges: that sometimes mountains are molehills and nothing more than that.

Sacrifice Play

BY

Sascha Zuger

Fifth grade had just ended, and my parents were sending me to a week of sleepaway camp. My big brother had told me stories about his previous summers there. I'd waited years to witness the magic of ticks exploding in a campfire, and was beside myself with joy.

Camp was everything I'd imagined and more. Not understanding the homesickness thing, I stuffed letters from Mom and Dad unread into my duffle bag. I had to attend to more important matters, like braiding the world's longest lanyard. By the end of the week, I was resolute: Camp simply could not be over for me. I waited for my parents, hoping they wouldn't be too mad about making the three-and-a-half-hour trip for nothing.

I'd like to say my reaction was mature as they led me to the car. But I was 10, and suffering my first heartbreak. Having no concept of how another week of camp would strain family finances, I ranted at the unfairness. My mom didn't see why I was so upset; she offered upbeat talk of next year's session. My dad seemed to feel my pain. He stared straight ahead, looking sadder as the miles passed.

My parents' opposite reactions likely stemmed from their backgrounds. Camp was a summer staple in Mom's family, no big deal. Dad grew up in the south suburbs of Chicago—the kind of place where you married a girl from the neighborhood and moved in across the street from your parents. Going away for a week, much less to some camp in the woods, was, to his parents, no sane way to spend money.

> The common wisdom is that you appreciate parental sacrifice only after you become a parent yourself.

Instead, he'd spent summers pursuing his boyhood passion—collecting baseball cards. And he never let go of a single one. For a guy who went to the office at 5:00 A.M. and returned every night in time for dinner, the cards must have been a precious reminder of the days when he played ball in the street and dreamed of lucking into the rarest Mickey Mantle rookie edition. In the same spirit, I dreamed of knotting macramé owls and winning at color wars.

Once home, I locked myself in my room and sobbed into my unpacked duffel bag. Dad knocked on my bedroom door a few hours later. When he invited me along to the collector's shop, I figured it was just a pathetic attempt to get my mind off s'mores. He approached the counter with a dusty old box in his hands. I looked up from a rack of movie posters when the collector's voice rose with excitement. He shoved a wad of bills into my father's hands. Dad handed over something small and flat in a plastic sheath and put the lid back on his box. Then he turned and led me out of the shop with a smile. "Let's go get ready for camp," he said. It was the happiest moment of my young life.

The common wisdom is that you appreciate parental sacrifice only after you become a parent yourself. It first dawned on me that I owed my father a debt when I saw the prices of baseball collectibles rise above six figures on eBay. I've been afraid to ask him which Mickey card he sold that day. One thing I know for sure: When he went to bat for me, it was an unquestionable home run.

You Can't Take it With You

BY

Maeve
Binchy

When I was 21, my father gave me 100 pounds (about $300) as a birthday present. It was a dizzying sum in the early 1960s, almost half my year's salary as a teacher. A generous man, my father thought it was a mistake to get tied up with the notion of money. It couldn't buy happiness. As a lawyer arguing trusts and bequests and having seen families and friendships torn apart over money, he had little respect for wealth in itself. The great thing to remember, he explained, was that you can't take it with you, so there's no point in holding on to it feverishly.

He needn't have worried too much about me. The money was all gone very quickly. But I remembered what he said about not being able to take it with you, and, in a way, that has directed my life ever since.

When I had been teaching for seven years, I got the ache to see the world and try something different. So I plunged into the job of freelance writer. Many of my friends thought I was quite insane to give up a good post in a good school. What would I do when I was old and gray and had nothing to live on, no nest egg? *Nest egg.* I liked neither the words nor the concept. My beloved parents had died, and I now lived in a rather falling-down apartment in Dublin. But I wasn't interested in possessions. If ever someone wanted something of mine, I gave it away. If you admired my good new pen, you should have it—a cheap ballpoint would do for me. (I wasn't completely selfless. Sometimes I gave people things I really needed, like my watch: I was turning up late everywhere and just had to ask for it back!)

> My father reminded us not to get tied up over having money. He needn't have worried about me.

People seemed delighted when you gave them things, and holding on to them didn't really matter to me. I worried more about love, or the lack of it. By now, I was 33 and the women's editor of the *Irish Times.* But I was always falling for wildly unsuitable people. Then I went and fell in love with a man who was unsuitable only in that he lived in England. So again I gave up a great job and went off to London to pursue him, followed all the way by a chorus of disapproving cluck, cluck, clucks. But we got married, and

The author, standing, third from left, with her family, circa 1960

it all turned out well. I tried writing fiction and, amazingly, was very successful at it.

Now that my husband and I had real money, we decided we had better make our wills. My husband is a man who doesn't care if we have solid silver forks or just some thing nice and practical to eat with. We got so excited at the thought of people one day having this or that, we said, Why shouldn't they have it now instead? So one of my friends wears the amethyst brooch that was given to me by my mother's aunt, and another pours cream from a 1938 silver jug that my parents received as a wedding gift. Just seeing their faces, we knew we were right not to wait.

Life is full of chance. How lucky, then, that my parents understood that you can't take it with you—and that you don't have to surround yourself with beautiful stylish things to live richly.

Children

Mad About the Boy

BY
Liz Smith

I've been married twice but never had children. To be honest, I was used to leading a childless existence: I'd admire babies on the street, then go on my way and enjoy my sophisticated, adult pursuits. I thought I was happy and successful. I had a full life with many friends.

Then, seven years ago, a young friend had a baby and made me the godmother. I was at the hospital when he arrived, and I've never forgotten the first time I saw him. He was wearing a little knit cap against the cold. It was the moment when my entire life changed.

I decided to take being a godmother seriously. This introduction of a baby, who then became a little boy, into my life was like water coming to the desert. I now know the ins and outs of preschools, babysitters, homework, and birthday parties. I have seen every Walt Disney movie, as well as nearly everything on the Cartoon Network and the Discovery Channel. I find myself reading bedtime stories in a dim light, listening to his evening prayers, rooting for the Yankees, and saving money for his college tuition. My life is filled with Halloween costumes, the Macy's Thanksgiving Day Parade, and visits to Santa—as well as countless soccer balls, bikes, and dinosaurs. I can assemble toys in rapid-fire motion, and I understand the crucial importance of having AA and AAA batteries on hand at all times. I am a whiz at Candy Land. I never realized how much I was missing without all these things in my life.

> I thought I'd seen it all, but I hadn't—because until my godson, I hadn't seen it through the eyes of a child.

Truth be told, I'm afraid I now prefer the company of a bright seven-year-old to that of the exquisite grown-ups in my life. I thought I'd seen it all, but I hadn't—because until my godson, I hadn't seen it through the eyes of a child. He is a museum enthusiast, and so I have relearned all the magic of New York City's Museum of Natural History, among others. I'm a lifelong gossip columnist, yet I now search the entertainment pages not to get dirt on Brad, Angelina, or Paris—but to find out which kid-friendly movies and plays I might be able to take my boy to see.

Keeping up with a child isn't relaxing. It's demanding. But I do feel blessed: The joy of witnessing him figure something out for the first time, the beauty of seeing the little stranger in a goalie mask make a great save, the glee

Smith gets a hug from her godson, Spencer.

of watching his shark imitations while he menaces me in the pool—it is all too thrilling.

I am the Lizzie in his life. He is the heart in mine.

A Place for Ethan

BY

Cammie
McGovern

Having a child with autism means working hard to seem as if you're just fine. When asked how you're doing, you tell a handful of stories that gloss over the worst of it. So when my friend Carrie asked if I would help her start an after-school play center for kids like Ethan, my then-six-year-old, I wanted to say no: For so long, it had felt important not to be defined as the parent of a child with special needs. Why start a club announcing the fact?

Eventually, I agreed, for purely selfish reasons. Carrie's oldest son played and taught drums, an instrument Ethan was desperate to try, though he'd panicked and withdrawn from every "real" teacher we took him to. With Carrie's son, a kind and unflappable teenager, Ethan came alive.

I'll help for six months, I thought, *and when Ethan gets tired of the drum lessons, I'll ease my way out.* Then an interesting thing happened. Carrie and I met with other parents to plan the Whole Children Center. And between talk of fund-raising and equipment purchasing, we started telling one another some real stories about our kids—the ones I'd always hesitated to tell. There were stories of horrible public scenes, battles for services, medical difficulties. And also this: the funny things our children had finally started to say and do.

> I've learned that sharing the hardest thing in my life can diminish the pain.

Through this group, I've learned that sharing the hardest thing in my life can diminish the pain. Also, that operating a nonprofit center is unbelievably difficult, and there is never enough money. But this no longer feels like a club we don't want to be part of. It's a haven, a place for our children to be themselves, to laugh and play, and for us parents to follow *their* lead for once.

Through the well-placed window in the lobby, I see Ethan and another boy making friends over red rubber balls they roll into each other. Without his leg braces, the other boy walks on his knees. A huge, toothy smile erupts every time a ball bounces into him. It's a game; they're having fun, and it's possible—wonder of wonders—that my son initiated it.

The author and her son, Ethan.

For most of the parents at the center, life felt very unlucky for a long time. Now we stand around the window most afternoons, a horseshoe of wordless mothers, marveling and feeling blessed. We never thought we'd see this day: our children surprising us, making their own way, finding a place for themselves in the world. And when we tell one another how lucky we feel, we really mean it.

A Toddler Lost, and Found, in the Deep End

BY

Mike Leonard

It was a sidewalk seam that tripped her up. My 22-month-old granddaughter and I had been holding hands when her urge to skip free, if only for a few seconds, separated us. Now little Josie was lying face-first on the concrete.

The world went quiet. Briefly. By the time I'd picked her up, Josie was in full-blown cry mode. But she was fine. It was a minor stumble, with many more to come. Still, it was scary—a reminder of the tenuous grip we have on life. Josie's little hand slipped from mine, and in the blink of an eye, she was down.

My wife and I have four children, and a memory of our first baby girl, my daughter Megan, flooded my brain. Even as a toddler, she'd been her own person, independent but sweet. When she was about two, we went to a friend's house for a barbecue. There was a pool, and after dinner I played water basketball in the shallow end with the other men; my wife, Cathy, was inside with the other wives. It was dark. Someone threw the ball to me, but the pass sailed over my head and into the deep end. I pushed my feet against the side of the pool, propelling my body toward where the ball had landed. There was something ahead, obscuring one of the underwater lights. As I glided closer, I could see a dress waving in the currents. And little red sandals. Then I saw the face.

> Josie's little hand slipped from mine, and in the blink of an eye, she was down.

It was my daughter Megan. I grabbed her by the waist and quickly lifted her body above the surface. Water gushed out of her mouth. A few seconds later, she started crying. She must have fallen into the darkened corner of the deep end seconds before the ball flew over my head. What if that pass had been good? What if I'd caught it? I got out of the pool and stood in the shadows holding my little girl as tightly as I could.

In my experience, the path through family life is riddled with mistakes, occasional terrors, and many blessings. The little girl I pulled out of the pool that day is all grown up now—and the mother of the toddler who slipped on the concrete. For me, as a father and now a

grandfather, perhaps the greatest blessing in life is being able to recognize how often I've been blessed.

Good Sport

BY

*Jodi
Picoult*

Last winter, my middle son learned that life isn't fair. Jake is 14. He's a terrific kid, with a sharp sense of humor and a penchant for hockey. He's a goalie, which means those little black marks on his helmet are the places where the pucks hit him.

During last year's tryouts for his league's three ranked teams, he fully expected to be in the middle of the pack. The results were posted, and Jake was placed on the lowest team instead. The young goalie who was given precedence over him was a child whose parents had argued previously when their son made the lowest team, and threatened to leave the organization. When Jake found out, he was crushed. And why wouldn't he be? He'd outskated this other boy. "Why have a tryout," he said, "if they already know who they want?"

Ironically, it was Jake who had taught me all over again as an adult that justice is a rare commodity in this world.

When he was 5, his hearing started to deteriorate. An MRI showed a rare, benign tumor growing in his ear. In the middle of 10 surgeries in three years, we learned that Jake had a tumor in the other ear, too (sort of like winning the bad-luck lottery twice). By the time he was tumor free, he was profoundly deaf in his left ear and had marginal hearing in his right, which required him to wear a hearing aid.

> It was Jake who had taught me that justice is a rare commodity in this world.

I remember the moment when the doctor told us about the second tumor, in what we'd thought was Jake's healthy ear. After listening, I excused myself, walked past the nurses' station through the double doors to the elevators, and slammed my fist into the wall. Why Jake? Why *twice*? It just wasn't fair. But then again, who ever said it was supposed to be?

We spend our childhood reading stories in which the deserving poor girl gets the prince in the end; where only the righteous can slide the sword from the stone. But somehow, as we get older, those rules don't apply. The day I found out about Jake's second tumor, I waited until I'd stopped crying, then walked back to my son's hospital room and gave him a list of reasons why this was not the end of the world.

Let me tell you what happened last year with hockey: Jake played goalie on the lower team, and eventually, when he got to know the other players, it didn't matter that he was passed over. In the meantime, I admitted that the hardest part of watching my son learn that life isn't fair was the knowledge that I could not keep him from growing up.

Luckily, I could offer him this proven antidote: optimism. Three years ago, his doctor whittled a sliver of Jake's skull to the size of an auditory bone, inserted it with a wish and a prayer into his ear canal, and gave Jake back his hearing. Maybe if he decides to try out one day for the high school team, hockey politics will veer away from cronyism and towards meritocracy. We can't protect our kids forever, but we *can* arm them to face adulthood with grace, confidence, and the understanding that even though you can't control the hand you're dealt, you have to stay in the game.

Because who knows? One day, against the odds, you just might win.

after such a long time

ent was lovely, and I'm

looking forward to see

everyone again soon

lots of love

A Letter from my Daughter

BY

Elizabeth Berg

In the months after my divorce, I went through hard times with both of my daughters, then 15 and 20. Things were particularly bad with my older daughter, Julie—often, we couldn't even talk on the phone without hanging up on each other.

Gradually, things began to get better, but the wound was still deep for both of us. One day, almost two years after the divorce, I got a card from Julie. This is what it said:

Dear Mom,

For all the hard times we've gone through and for all the little things you hold so dear that you THINK you've failed to pass on, I want to assure you they have not gone unnoticed. When I was growing up and complaining bitterly about having to walk the few blocks to school, you were pointing out the value of nature and walks outside. You have taught me to reflect on life, to breathe in the

beautiful parts and breathe out the bad, to see the best in people. I still write thank-you cards. I still say please and thank you. I still smile under pressure. I still give people a second chance. I tip cabdrivers and waiters too much. I marvel at the sight of spring flowers and Christmas lights more than at jewelry and brand-name clothes. When I feel sick, I eat lots of fruits and vegetables and drink juice and take vitamin C. I think I was more upset when I helped a "fallen" woman up onto her ice skates than she was! And all of this I owe to you. I am a better person in many ways because of the many things you taught me—and I hope this card makes at least a humble attempt to convey that I love you, Mom.

> It was a blessing so profound, I still cannot read Julie's words without weeping.

What parent doesn't hope for this kind of acknowledgment? But for me, still swimming through an ocean of guilt and sadness, wondering if I'd ever reach the other side, it was a blessing so profound, I still cannot read Julie's words without weeping. Her message was a great gulp of air at a time when I needed it most. "The best things, the truest things, always make me cry," a friend of mine said recently. I guess that's true for me, too. In the ongoing adjustment

Author Elizabeth Berg, right, with daughter Julie

that divorce is, I have faith in the form of a card that says on the outside "Love bears all things, believes all things, hopes all things, endures all things. Love never ends." The message on the inside, written in my daughter's careful script, proves that it is so.

Family

My Other Family

BY

Cecile
Gilmer

I believe that families are not only blood relatives but sometimes people who just show up and love you when no one else will.

In May 1977, I was living in a Howard Johnson's motel off Interstate 10 in Houston. My dad and I shared a room with two double beds and a bathroom way too small for a modest 15-year-old girl and her father. Dad's second marriage was deteriorating, and my stepmother had kicked us both out of the house the previous week. Dad had no idea what to do with me.

That's when my "other" family showed up. Barbara and Roland Beach took me into their home because their only daughter, Su, my best friend, asked them to. I lived with them for the next seven years. Barb starched my drill team skirts, same as Su's. She made sure I had doctors' appointments, help with homework, Jordache jeans, and nightly hugs. She and Roland attended every football game when Su and I marched, every school play I performed in, even when I had no speaking lines. As far as I could tell, for the Beaches, there was no difference between Su and me…I was their daughter too.

When Su and I left for rival colleges, the Beaches kept my room the same for the entire four years I attended school. Recently, Barb gave me the insurance policy they'd bought when I first moved in with them and continued to pay on for 23 years, so I could cash it out.

> I'd also learned early on to rely only on myself and to view even those with good intentions as a little suspect.

My mother died of a self-inflicted gunshot wound when I was 7, and from then on, my father mostly relied on other people to raise my sister and brother and me. By the time I went to live with the Beaches, I believed that life was unfair and that love was untrustworthy.

With the Beaches, I came a long way in learning to open my heart, but it was not always my first inclination. I'd also learned early on to rely only on myself and to view even those with good intentions as a little suspect. When I became a young woman, I dated men, some decent and some who reinforced the indelible perception I had of the world as a terrible and frightening place. Each time I stumbled, the Beaches guided me back into the world, showing me that love can, if not overcome, then certainly assuage one's fears. Without them, I would have become a bitter, cynical woman.

After working in the hospitality industry for many years, I took a job at a university. Selling $15,000 hotel suites in Miami Beach had been a sexy endeavor, but it was a shadow to the joy I now find in raising money to support college students.

I've never married, but I have the Beaches and I always will. I believe in family. For me, it wasn't the family that was there on the day I was born. It was the one that was there for me when I was living in a Howard Johnson's on Interstate 10.

A Gift from my Brothers

BY

Molly O'Neill

My childhood was defined by a single, all-consuming desire. I wanted a baby sister, someone who adored me and understood me and who eagerly awaited my hand-me-downs. My mother promised! She'd always regretted her own lack of sisters: "I'm going to make sure you aren't lonely when you grow up," she said.

But she didn't keep her promise, at least not directly. From the time I was three until I was ten, she did nothing but deliver baby brothers. I did my best to persuade my mother's uterus to grow a girl. I waved pink things—blankets, hair ribbons, even the clothes I'd worn as an infant—around my mother like magical flags. Nothing worked.

Finally, when she'd delivered her fifth son, my mother stopped making promises. "Paul. That's all," she declared to my father.

The boys shattered the quiet order of our days and turned our home into a chaos of cowboys, Indians, Tonka toys, and cap guns. "It's beyond me!" my mother screamed.

My father shrugged.

> The boys shattered the quiet order of our days and turned our home into a chaos of Tonka toys and cap guns.

In retrospect, having brothers wasn't all bad. Many people spend their lives thinking that the opposite sex comes from the opposite end of the solar system. I grew up on the same planet with men, knowing that their foibles, appetites, and hearts were different from—but very much complementary to—my own. Because my brothers are funny and competitive, I've laughed more than any ten women I know. I also tend to think strategically as well as emotionally and have never been exploited by handymen. But it took me a long time to comprehend the true blessing of brothers: sisters-in-law!

For many years now, my brothers' wives have provided the tender sibling support I always dreamed of—choosing the discreetly oversize cashmere sweater for Christmas the year I gained weight, assembling a trove of expensive makeup to cheer me up after I'd had several miscarriages, sharing their children—"Why don't you call your Aunt

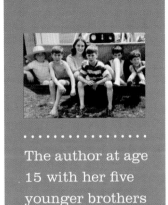

The author at age 15 with her five younger brothers

Molly?"—as my own bid for motherhood became less and less likely.

Our individual attachments vary, but the steady hum of us— the fasions we've debated, the diets we've tried, the walks we've taken, the stories we've shared, the meals we've cooked, the babies we've chased, the eyeballs we've raised to heaven over *Men!*—has rubbed away my old resentments. My brothers are an all but impenetrable fraternity; my sisters-in-law have become my sorority, showing me the blessing of belonging.

Knit Together

BY

*Kate
Jacobs*

Seven years ago, my husband, Jon, and I had a beautiful mid-October wedding. It was stressful, to be sure—coming, as it did, a month after the September 11 terrorist attacks—but wonderful. We'd been brave to go through with it, we decided. All would be well. At the time, Jon worked as tech director at a biotech startup in Pittsburgh and I was a magazine editor in Manhattan. It was an arrangement we'd managed throughout our engagement—every weekend becoming a romantic reunion—and would resume after a brief honeymoon.

The day we got home, Jon telephoned to let me know he'd just been laid off, thanks to the ripple effect from 9/11. In short order, he arrived in New York City, bringing with him his life—from childhood to the wedding—in boxes that had to be wedged into the already compact apartment I rented with a roommate. At least we're together in one city, we whispered to ourselves late at night. We'd be OK.

Three weeks after that, the magazine at which I was a senior editor folded. So there we were: the newlyweds, the roommate (who'd also been laid off), and the boxes.

Christmas loomed large. The year before, we'd spent lavishly—even the wrapping paper had been selected at a specialty store. We'd been ridiculous and we hadn't even known it.

> As we walked around, we felt liberated by the very fact of not being able to shop until we dropped.

But this was our first holiday as a married couple and we wanted it to be special. The gift "budget" I wrote out when I still had a job had become a joke; that money was going to be needed for real bills. So I bought Jon a bargain book and a pack of playing cards. He bought me the same, and a home-decor magazine, for the day when we'd have a home, he said, and our lives would be back on track.

December really is the best season in New York. As we walked around, we felt liberated by the very fact of not being able to shop until we dropped. And when, on Christmas morning, we opened our gifts at my parents' home in Canada (the tickets purchased with air miles), we spent more time watching everyone else. We laughed, for the first time in a long while, as we tucked into the turkey dinner.

In the months of job hunting that followed, though I'd never published fiction, I sketched out an idea for what will be my fourth novel. I didn't know that then. Instead, there were fights. Worry-filled nights. But that, then, was a surprise gift: We were a tight little duo now.

The double layoff renewed our approach to the holidays. These are the gifts we exchange: a bottle of good balsamic vinegar. Lounge-y pajamas. The scarf I knit, secretly, after Jon was asleep, surprising him on Christmas day. Even though we now live in California and have no need for scarves. The spirit of that first Christmas remains. There may be worse, we have learned, but there will also be better.

Open-Door Policy

BY

Elinor Lipman

For the first 12 years of my life, I lived in the smallest house on Cascade Avenue in Lowell, Massachusetts. Its five rooms fit us fine, I thought: My sister and I shared a room across the hall from my parents. We had no dining room or guest room, which meant visitors rarely crossed our threshold. But I didn't have to go far—six blocks—to experience an open-door side of life: the grand white Victorian that was Aunt Marion's boardinghouse.

To a shy little girl raised under glass, "rooms to let" was thrilling and near-incredible: Perfect strangers lived upstairs, sleeping on family sheets and pillows, in possession of a front-door key. Auntie Marion was my mother's older sister, a sunny, affectionate, aproned woman, who never failed to greet her n ieces' frequent arrivals with her arms wide open. She and Uncle Lenny, a shoe salesman, were not rich; they'd bought the queen-size edifice for its income potential.

The boarders, many of them refugees from post-World War II Europe, were mostly sent by the Lowell Textile Institute housing office. They could have been monks or CIA operatives—so quiet, so neat, so buttoned-down and well behaved—or so it appeared to me, the awe-struck child. The house itself had me in its thrall: its double front doors, stained glass windows, and hitching post out front. I knew every inch, not from snooping, but as a devoted visitor, delighted to trail after Aunt Marion, playing junior chambermaid, as she dusted knickknacks on the mantel, made the beds, and cleaned the bathroom (ammonia, always). She never scolded, never once said, "No, sorry, not a good time for you to drop by."

My elementary school was closer to her house than my own, and no lunch date delighted me more than the one in Aunt Marion's kitchen. During holiday meals, she shrugged away differences of opinion with her homey, philosophical, "That's why they have chocolate and vanilla." Long before "role model" came into popular usage, she represented all the term encompasses to a youngster whose own mother could be a little aloof to strangers. She was friendly to all, a hostess so obliging that she baked her cakes and kugels half with raisins, half without, to please all tastes.

Though I resemble the other side of the family, my father's, there's no higher compliment than being told I remind someone of Aunt Marion—which I translate as, "Woman who keeps her bad moods to herself." I seem to have inherited not only her recipe for rugelach, but also a rooming house inclination, in place of my parents' "no vacancy" policy. And when a friend or acquaintance (OK, relative stranger) writes, "Coming through town! Would love to see you/meet you/grab a cup of coffee," a beloved voice from my past almost always prompts me to ask, "Do you need a bed?"

Last First Kiss

BY

Kelly
Corrigan

I was raised as girls of my era were, with Debutante Ball Barbie, Bonne Bell Lip Smackers, and *Love Boat*. I spent a lot of time pulling together pink boas and high heels and sparkly plastic earrings, then taking the whole fantastic ensemble slowly down the stairs to show my parents, who'd tilt their heads to the side and declare me a "beautiful" princess. And, well, I believed them.

Eventually, of course, I abandoned dress-ups. But I did not abandon the idea that something terribly romantic was in store for me.

When I moved to San Francisco in my early 20s, the streets were littered with Price Charmings in fleece pullovers, and a thing called the Internet was filling the air with the mouthwatering scent of preposterous riches. The elaborate ballgown and grand staircase, the orchestra and the scurrying staff—these fairy-tale staples hardly seemed far-fetched.

After a few years, I found a keeper in the kitchen of my friend's house, pouring himself a glass of Merlot and offering to refill mine. After some chatter, Edward told me that he had just taken a job with Teleworld, in Silicon Valley. Teleworld, he explained, was going to change television forever and he was the 28th employee. He'd bought his stock options on his first day for four cents apiece.

Three dates later, in this era of great expectations, I was made weak and rosy-cheeked by my last first kiss ever. Within a year, I became a wife, Teleworld became TiVo, and checking our options became an aphrodisiac. My romantic something was, at last, at hand.

It shames me to admit what I thought that something might be but, for sure, it included decorators, board meetings, a personal chef, and commissioned artwork. Plus, four kids who all looked alike and loved one another like the Kennedys. Oh, and parents' weekends at various Ivy League schools.

Then one Thursday night a few years ago, my husband totaled his car on the way home from work. He was unharmed but electric with shock. Not much later, my cousin's teenage son died in a car accident, a mile from his front door. And then, I found a seven-centimeter tumor—the size of a baseball—in my breast one night while taking a bubble bath with my two little girls who don't look at all alike and squabble twenty-some times a day.

I got better and as I did, a new fantasy emerged—a fantasy so outrageous I hesitate to say it out loud: me on my IKEA couch, with that bluish hair old ladies sometimes get, opening the mail to find snapshots of my grandchildren riding bikes or ice-skating or just sitting there looking like regular, healthy kids who hate posing for photos, and Edward, my last first kiss ever, still sitting beside me.

Blood is Thicker than Water

BY

Cathleen
Schine

When I was a child, and my grandparents would arrive at our home in their baby blue Buick, my brother and I would run to greet them the way other children ran to greet the Good Humor truck. My grandfather would honk the horn, and we would race like maniacs, doors slamming behind us. Partly, we were excited to see them, of course. But that honking meant the same thing to us as the tinkling of the ice cream truck—good things to eat.

The minute they got out of the car, my grandmother would open the trunk and retrieve a shoebox held shut by a rubber band. Inside, wrapped in waxed paper (plastic wrap in later years), would be layers and layers of brownies, stacked like bricks. She would hand them over with great ceremony and say, "These are for blood." We were not allowed to share our brownies with friends. Not even our best friends and next-door neighbors Wendy and David, whose grandmother always gave us her butter cookies. Brownies, and every other good thing, were reserved for blood.

For my grandmother, blood was far thicker than water. She grew up in a family of four brothers and four sisters; her aunt and uncle lived next door. When my grandmother married my grandfather during the Depression, they made their first home with all those siblings, not to mention my great-grandparents. And while he traveled selling plumbing supplies, she stayed put. Is it any wonder the brownies were meant to stay home, as well?

How had the miser of baked goods become so openhanded?

My grandmother never had many friends, and didn't really need them. All those sisters, so safe to gossip with, to argue and feud and make up with. Even after she and my grandfather moved out of the big house, she was never too lonely. Two of her sisters moved nearby, and soon enough, my great-grandmother—a gentle soul in contrast to my rather wacky grandmother—moved in with them. Blood was thick indeed in that family. But as the years wore on, my grandmother's mother, husband, and siblings all died, leaving her alone. When she moved to New York to be near my mother, my aunt, and the grandchildren, it became painfully apparent, to us and to her, that Grandma didn't know how to make friends. She'd never had to. She still made brownies, though.

To keep Grandma from getting too lonely, we invited her to dinner and introduced her to our friends. Soon, a strange and wonderful phenomenon took place. When Grandma invited us to tea, she invited our friends as well! My friend Nancy, who still talks about the sliver of Grandma's cheesecake I slipped her in fourth grade, was actually offered a whole piece—on a plate! Sometimes Grandma would hand me a Ziploc bag of Toll House cookies and make me swear I would pass them on to some particular friend. It was a little scary, this transformation. How had the miser of baked goods—the woman who would have liked to perform DNA tests before serving sponge cake— become so openhanded? Evolution, I think. She changed because she had to. In her 80s, Grandma reinvented herself as a true New Yorker, striding down the street, greeting shopkeepers who, to my astonishment, all knew her name. With her knack for self-preservation, my clever and adaptable grandmother revealed the limits of a proverb: She discovered that, sometimes, family resides in friendship.

Nourishment

Here's to You, Mrs. Berenson

BY

Chitra
Banerjee
Divakaruni

It was a blustery evening in Chicago. The wind pierced through the neon-orange coat I'd bought with high hopes in Calcutta, my hometown, just a month before. Here, people in sober browns and black eyed it—and the sari I wore under it—with silent suspicion. Finally, the bus appeared around the corner. I boarded and sank into my seat thankfully.

I was 19, and the toddler whom I babysat had been cranky all day. Soon, though, I'd be back at the apartment where I was staying with relatives. In a few hours, after dinner and comedy shows with indecipherable jokes, I'd be able to pull out the sofa bed and crawl into it.

Just then, the bus shuddered to a stop. The engine was dead, the driver said. Maybe, I thought as I trudged along the sidewalk, I should give up my dream, go back to India. Agree to an arranged marriage like my cousin. Then I saw the small, brightly lit building with its American flag and sign in front: "Library." It looked so warm inside, I couldn't resist, though I knew my relatives would worry.

The women at the desk—an older lady—gave a welcoming nod. A tag pinned to her cardigan said "A. Berenson, Librarian." Feeling bold, I asked if I could borrow a book. She asked if I had identification. I produced it, and she typed out a card with my name on it. When I asked how many books I could take home, she said, "As many as you can carry out! What are you looking for?" Her interest was so genuine that, before I knew it, I was confiding my dream: "I want to go to college and study American literature." She led me to the stacks, paused, then handed me *The Great Gatsby.* I'd never heard of it, but already I trusted Mrs. Berenson.

> Her interest was so genuine that, before I knew it, I was confiding my dream.

That night, I plunged into a fascinating world of affluence and excess. My own problems receded as I waited tensely to see if Gatsby would find love. Later, when I expressed outrage that he'd been killed, Mrs. B. smiled and said, "But it's made you care. Isn't that what counts?"

Over the next months, Mrs. B. gave me many more books and—"because fun is important"—introduced me to her favorite singers, from Billie Holiday to Simon and

Garfunkel. Perhaps because she took my opinions seriously, I put aside my pride, borrowed money from relatives, and got my degrees. I started to teach. Began to write. In all that busyness, Mrs. B. slipped into the cracks of my memory.

Years later, when my first book was published, I walked into our local library—a place my children loved as much as I did. There is was, my book, nestled between Dickinson and Dybek. And suddenly I was back in those other stacks, and Mrs. B. was smiling at me. Words I never got a chance to tell her flowed into my mind: *God bless you please, Mrs. Berenson, I owe you more than I can ever say.* And then, because fun is important: *Hey, hey, hey.*

Flavor of Home

BY

Elmaz Abinader

My sisters and I loved to spin—our arms out to the side and the skirts of our school uniforms lifting. When my mother called *"Tai houn!"* through the window, our flights froze. *Come here!* We barely understood Arabic but dropped our arms and rushed to the kitchen.

As we stood in a line, Mother handed each of us a big brown paper bag from the supermarket. It was grape-leaf-collection day, the moment in spring when the leaves are most tender. My sisters and I would have to walk through our Pennsylvania town asking neighbors if we could pick leaves from their vines. We were already considered odd because of our father's strong accent, our old-country habits. Now, as leaf panhandlers traipsing from one street to another, peeking into backyards and knocking on doors, our strangeness was amplified, and mortified me.

My mother drew a small circle in her palm. "No bigger than this," she said. "Always pick the third one from the end—I don't want any tough leaves." My sisters and I set out for Cannon Hill, where we knew many yards had ornamental grapevines knotted around white trellises. I braced myself for the incredulous looks from people when we explained that we *ate* them.

> Though I was miles from home, I couldn't shake the flavors of my childhood.

Back then, the early 1960s, most Americans didn't know where Lebanon was and certainly hadn't tasted our food. My mother tried to make it sound appetizing when her clubs met at our house. She called hummus "Tangy Dip," and tabbouleh "Summer Salad." But the dishes seemed like goop to her visitors. "You *eat* that?" they asked. The buffet that lay before them took hours of preparation. My sisters and I, our grandmother and mother, sat at our yellow kitchen table, filling fresh grape leaves with rice and lamb and spices we ground ourselves. Our mother's *warak inhab* were tight and neat—a finger-size representation of our humiliation and hard work.

After college, I took a corporate job in New York City. When my mother came to visit, I suggested we eat dinner at my favorite health food restaurant. She wrinkled her nose.

"You'll like the food," I promised. As she held the menu, I watched her eyes travel down the columns. She began to giggle. "Mom," I whispered. "What's so funny?" She lifted her head from behind the menu. "This isn't *health* food," she said. "It's our food!" Sure enough, there were hummus and stuffed grape leaves and tabbouleh. She'd found me out. Though I was miles from home, I couldn't shake the flavors of my childhood—or the rituals, it turned out.

Now, in California, I'm an unapologetic grape-leaf forager, pestering my neighbors each spring. I count the third leaf from the end, measure it against my palm, and pluck it to put in my bag. No one asks what I'm going to do with them. When I get the itch to make *warak inhab,* I invite my girlfriends over for the afternoon. We sit around my kitchen table, talking and rolling, absorbing the fragrances of lemon, garlic, and cinnamon—the scents of home.

Big Love

BY
Rachel Balducci

Shortly after my husband and I told our families we were expecting baby number five, my father-in-law stopped by the house with a dozen donuts. Buelo (as Paul's dad is known) had been out grocery shopping early and found the store's yeast donuts on sale. He thought the boys and I would enjoy the treat, so he bought some for us.

"These are my absolute favorite," I declared. "Thank you so much!" He left, and the boys and I dove into the sugary goodness.

The next day, there was a knock at the door. Again it was Paul's dad, with another dozen of those too-delicious yeast donuts.

"Thank you again," I said. And I meant it. My favorite donuts—two days in a row!

The third morning, Mr. B. did not stop by, and I must say I was relieved. *Because I just can't say no to you, Donut.* Plus, all that sugar was making me dizzy. But Day Four brought another knock and another dozen donuts to the back door. "Mr. B.," I said, "are you trying to fatten me up?"

The donut spree ended after that, though every couple of months Paul's dad will still come calling out of the blue with a batch of you-know-what. It's a simple thing, but it means so much that my father-in-law remembers this tiny detail—something he knows I really enjoy—to show he cares.

> While, in theory, I strive to love others as myself, it had never occurred to me that I should do it extravagantly.

His thoughtfulness reminds me of a phrase translated from Corinthians 13:13, "Love extravagantly." The first time I heard the line, it stopped me in my tracks. While, in theory, I strive to love others as myself, it had never occurred to me that I should do it *extravagantly*. Of course, that doesn't mean with expensive gifts or melodrama. Instead, it's showing love without counting cost—a kind deed for someone just because. For my father-in-law, there's no hidden agenda when he brings donuts. He just knows we really (really!) like them.

Sometimes, I'll admit, showing the same consideration at home requires a bit of amnesia; it means giving everything and holding back nothing, like the memory of a past disappointment or aggravation. It's repairing wrongdoing and then starting over fresh—with my kids and especially with Paul. Loving extravagantly can be as simple as putting away his laundry, or conversely, Paul picking up dinner on the way home because I'm exhausted and need the night off.

In life, we have so many opportunities to show others we love them. Some call for grand gestures, but the rest of the time, it's the little things—repeated over and over—that make us feel cared for and deeply touch our hearts.

In the months since Henry's birth last July, our family has received many sweet gifts of love. When my father-in-law came to the hospital to meet his newest grandson, he didn't bring donuts. But a few weeks later, I answered a knock at the door and there was Buelo with his treat. "For the boys," he said. "And the baby." And for me.

The Secret Ingredient

BY

Jan Barker

The first thing I did when Cameron, my 12-year-old, broke her ankle was bake. Well, maybe not the *first* thing. First I consoled her, then I called the orthopedist, and then I consulted my cookbooks.

Cam fell off a horse during a weekend visit with her dad, my ex-husband, and she called me on her way to the hospital. It was the end of her summer fun—or so she thought, as she sobbed on the phone. "It'll be OK," I reassured her, heading to the kitchen. "Bones heal and the horse is fine."

I've baked all my life and was trained by an expert— my paternal grandmother in Alabama. Her kitchen, with its blue gingham curtains and speckled Formica counter-top, was more than just a place to prepare meals. It was a sanctuary. My mother, while a wonderful woman, was a disaster in the kitchen. She suffered from manic depression and baking was simply beyond her.

Sad, but it's also why Grandma's kitchen was where I felt happiest in the world. "Come help," she'd say when I visited every summer, and I'd stand between her and her Sunbeam mixer, sticking my fingers in the batter after each addition. As a finishing touch, I'd pour in the vanilla she bought at the pharmacy counter as if it were contraband. "I don't use that junk they sell in the grocery," she told me. "It tastes like nothin'." I came to love the scent of vanilla so much I used it as perfume when I was a teenager. Every Southern girl, I thought, should smell like cake.

In our fractured family, baking really means love.

When Cam hobbled through the door on her crutches, she went straight to the kitchen. My creation had the desired effect—her eyes lit up and her dimples appeared when she spotted the Coca-Cola cake on the counter. "I knew you were going to bake me something," she said.

She sat at the kitchen table with a big slice and a glass of milk and told me all about her accident—how another rider had cantered right into her as she went over a jump, and she'd gone flying. The more she talked and ate, the better she felt. The cake sat on the table between us, as much symbol as sweet treat. In our fractured family, baking really means love.

To even things up, I decided to surprise her older sister, Ali, with a mocha cake. One of Ali's fondest memories is of the chocolate peanut butter cookies Grandma had waiting for her in the dining room every time we visited. We bake them every year at Christmas. And when we put them into the oven, I do what Grandma did when I was little—leave lots of batter in the bowl and hand it to the child.

This summer, when I asked Ali if she wanted me to bake some Great-Grandma cookies, she said no. "If we have them all the time," she explained, "they won't be special."

I don't know what makes them so tasty. Maybe it's the Mexican vanilla I use, or how I bump up the baking soda the way Grandma used to do so they'll be extra light.

Or maybe it's just the love.

Farewell My Lovelies

BY

Jessica Queller

I f someone had told me at 30 that in the next five years I would have my breasts removed in a preemptive strike against cancer, I'd have called her crazy. What a difference five years make.

Eleven months after my mother died, I tested positive for the same genetic mutation that had caused her early breast cancer and the ovarian cancer that finally killed her. Although I was 35 and single, the idea of undergoing a double mastectomy to protect myself from cancer no longer seemed insane. In fact, after watching my young, vibrant mother die a horrific death, it seemed the logical choice. Some members of my family worried about me. They believed I was wildly underestimating how traumatized I'd be when I woke up without my breasts. I decided to have the operations because—for me—reconstructed breasts were preferable to cancer. And yet I expected this would be a deeply mournful period of my life.

It turned out to be one of the most joyous. In those final days before the surgery, I was in a feverish, almost elated state. I'd always envisioned my friends gathering to spoil me before my wedding. Instead, I had a "farewell breasts" night out with eight of my closest girlfriends. In lipstick and heels, we met at a chic bistro in Manhattan's meatpacking district, drank cosmopolitans, and laughed with abandon. Each friend gave a long, emotional toast in my honor. To all appearances, we were a bachelorette party—and I was the bride.

> I blinked in amazement as the deliverymen carried in tree after beautiful tree, breathing new life into my home.

The week before my mastectomy, my father and sister went to a nursery and bought seven large trees for me as a gift—three for inside my apartment, and four to put outside on the small terrace. I blinked in amazement as the deliverymen carried in tree after beautiful tree, breathing new life into my home. The loved ones in my life surrounded and buoyed me—they made me feel special and courageous.

The first week home post-surgery, I was high on Vicodin and had drainage tubes pinned to my cotton nightie, yet I was hostess to an endless stream of visitors in what felt like an around-the-clock party. I overdid it, of course, and my doctor soon shut down the festivities.

Two weeks after surgery, I went in to see Dr. Roses for an exam. He held the pathology report in his hand. "You had precancerous changes in your right breast tissue, Jessica. Atypical ductal hyperplasia."

I'd felt certain my breasts needed to be sacrificed for my health, but I hadn't been expecting *this*. The doctor registered the shock and disbelief on my face. "If you had any doubt about the course of action you chose, this should dispel it. You did the right thing."

Two years post-surgery, though, my strongest memory is being showered with love from the extraordinary people in my life. I've learned that the most devastating experience—even losing a mother to a terrible disease—can glimmer with surprising rays of hope.

Friendship

Wrapped in Love

BY

Ann Hood

A week before my husband and I left for China to adopt our daughter Annabelle, my friend Mary called. "Do you know what I need?" she asked. "A girls' night out." Since I was about to become the mother of a ten-month-old, the idea sounded especially good. Mary promised to pick me up on Tuesday at seven. "Sarah's coming too," she added.

"Great," I said, though I hadn't realized Sarah and Mary were also acquainted.

Tuesday night, I put on my favorite sparkly skirt, anticipating dinner at some chic local spot. "Where are we going?" I asked after climbing into Mary's Volvo. "I know a good Chinese restaurant," Sarah volunteered. Mary added, "I'm so sick of the usual places." I was about to spend two weeks eating nothing but Chinese food, but I didn't want to be a spoilsport.

The place was empty when we got there, except for some women way in the back. I was starting to feel ridiculous in my sparkly skirt. Then I recognized my friend Ruthie across the room. She was talking to someone who looked like my friend Laurie. And beside Ruthie was my friend Frances. Now they were waving at me and grinning, Frances and Laurie and Ruthie. With them were Amy, Jennifer, and Nancy.

> Everyone started talking, pointing out who had knit what and which stitches they'd used.

Reading the confused look on my face, Laurie said: "What do we all have in common?"

Finally, it came to me.

"We all knit," I said. Then Laurie handed me a box, from which I took a baby blanket made of dozens of knit squares. These friends, these women who had only knitting and me in common, had secretly been meeting for six months—ever since they had seen the picture of our baby. They had knit her a blanket.

I remembered a night during a snowstorm when I had stopped at Nancy's to use her phone and she had acted as if she didn't want me to come in.

"The squares were all laid out!" she explained. "I didn't want you to see!"

Everyone started talking, pointing out who had knit what and which stitches they'd used. There was a fluffy white swan for the White Swan Hotel in China, where all adopting parents stay. And a snaking red thread, symbolizing the thread that, in Chinese legend, links parents to children.

I spread the blanket open on my lap and ran my fingers across the soft wool. How blessed I was to have these friends…and what a blessing that they'd found one another! A baby 6,000 miles away had brought them together to share in the excitement and wonder of her arrival. They had knit their love for me and for her with each stitch.

Soon my daughter would be wrapped in the blanket, and I would be whispering to her: *Frances knit the chili pepper, Ruthie made the teddy bear, and Louise connected the pieces— connecting all of us, forever.*

A Friend in Need is a Friend Indeed

BY

Elizabeth Berg

Thirty years ago, when I met my friend John, he was an advertising executive who wore designer suits and drove a fancy English car. But one day he decided he'd had enough of city life and became a homesteader in New Hampshire. He never again wore a suit, attended a meeting, or cashed a paycheck from a corporation. He sent me letters about making maple syrup, jury-rigging his truck, and eating sweet peas right off the vine in his garden.

Once, when I had business in a nearby city, I went to visit him in the house he'd built with his own two hands. When I arrived (after traveling miles over a bumpy dirt road that nearly loosened my fillings), I stood turning in slow circles in his kitchen, amazed. The cabin was small but very beautiful, with stained glass windows, a sleeping loft with exposed beams, comfortable armchairs, and a cast-iron stove, which he used to make homemade applesauce and whole wheat bread. He had a radio and a tape recorder duct-taped together, for listening to books on tape while he worked or drove. That, along with good conversation and the changing seasons, was his entertainment.

> Someone once said that the good part about helping a friend in need is that it shows you your finest self.

Some years later, I got a call from John's brother. John was in the hospital, having been diagnosed with inoperable brain cancer.

John endured treatments that didn't help; he failed quickly; he cast about for words; he sometimes wet his pants; toward the end, he fell down a lot. It became difficult for some people to be with him. A mutual friend declined to visit, saying, "I just don't know what to say."

I could understand this response; it was hard, at first. Scary. Heartbreaking. But still.

The last time I visited John before he went into hospice, it was a beautiful summer day, and he was sitting out on a porch in his wheelchair, having lunch with friends at a large wooden table. The food was glorious, and people laughed hard and talked loudly and helped John eat and take his many pills. In their eyes was great love and also great commitment: They would stand by him, just like always, only more so. I doubt I'll ever feel more privileged to be part of a group.

The author with John, in 1988.

After lunch, John gazed longingly at a pond where he'd often swum. I pushed him as close as his wheelchair would go, then went the rest of the way to the edge of the pond myself. I cupped my hands to fill them with water, then crouched before John to pour it over his legs. I looked up at him and he smiled, a moment of wide acknowledgment and gratitude for the love of his friends, for the feel of cool water on a hot summer day, for being alive on Earth and still able and willing to take the gifts it offered.

It is no exaggeration to say that he showed me how to die a good death.

Someone once said that the good part about helping a friend in need is that it shows you your finest self. I would add this: Even when the circumstances are not so dire, to present a caring self to one who is in need will invariably give you back far more than you give.

Adopting Katie

BY

*Melinda
Santa Cruz*

I'd endured breast cancer treatments for almost a year when I decided to volunteer at my local animal shelter. Dogs are my true passion, but the homeowners association where we live forbade them, and I longed to run my fingers through soft fur and to smile into the adoring eyes of puppies.

After two months at the shelter, I had seen many dogs come and go, but one senior dog remained unclaimed. An Akita mix named Katie, she was slow and cloudy-eyed. Shelter workers said she had "bossy old broad syndrome," because she'd lie down on her walks and refuse to budge; once she had even urinated on the face of another dog.

Her personality wasn't the most charismatic, but Katie exuded a sweetness that captured the hearts of both volunteers and staff members. When the kennel filled to capacity, the staff decided to put her in a pen with another dog, rather than put her down. Katie got along well with her kennel mate, and everyone was happy.

One day, I came home to find a notice that said the association rules had changed, and each family would now be allowed to keep one dog. My head quickly filled with the many possibilities. Like most people, I preferred to adopt a frolicking puppy or a gorgeous purebred. But then I thought about old, gentle Katie, and my mind was made up. I would bring her home the next day.

> At night, Katie slept on my feet or with a paw spread over my legs, as if to make sure I'd still be there when she woke up.

Staff members cried upon hearing that Katie was my choice. As I was leaving, a visitor glared at me in the shelter lobby but then apologized when she realized I was taking old Katie out, not bringing her in.

Katie rode home in the backseat of my car, resting her chin on the upraised armrest so that her face got the full blast of air-conditioning. It must have been heaven after months of sweltering heat at the shelter. When we got home, she sniffed around and kept her distance as I patted the couch beside me. Minutes later, when she finally leaped up, I knew she had made the decision to stay. A curtain of darkness lifted, and I experienced true joy for the first time since my cancer diagnosis.

At night, Katie slept on my feet or with a paw spread over my legs, as if to make sure I'd still be there when she woke up. I didn't buy a leash; she happily followed me anywhere. I considered her such a blessing that each night I kissed her on the head and said, "Thank God for you," before going to bed. Eventually, Katie's devotion inspired me to take a dog-training instructor's course, which proved to be a bigger challenge than I'd bargained for.

Late one night, I was lying on the couch, pouring over a textbook in preparation for a test, when Katie appeared beside me. When I turned my face toward her, she licked me on the forehead, then circled and plopped down on the bed. I'd been so consumed with studying, I'd forgotten about our ritual.

Katie has taught me that unconditional love doesn't have to come in the most appealing package. She may not be the dog I wanted, but I'm certain she's the dog God wanted me to have.

I Love You up to the Sky

BY

Jacquelyn Mitchard

We met 22 years ago, when she cut my hair. Stacey was just out of cosmetology school. My son was a toddler who politely touched the stars on the salon's Christmas tree with one finger—a gesture that charmed her no end. For a new mom, well, she had me at hello.

Stacey had dozens of friends; most of them confided in *her*. In me, she seemed to find someone *she* could turn to. Over pizza, we shared our wonder at the unpredictability of life, men, and bosses. I loved her voice. It was gravelly and sexy, like an aging lounge signer's.

"If I die," I told my husband, Dan, "you have to marry Stacey. She's funny and beautiful and loves the kids and has the best voice on earth."

Instead, it was Dan who died, of colon cancer. He was barely into his 40s.

A year after his death, with three sons I could barely support, I decided to adopt a baby girl. Those who thought I was only mildly insane before decided I'd lost it completely. Yet Stacey supported me. She adored Francie and was the dearest "auntie" my little girl had.

> Stacey's voice on tape sent a reminder that her love for us was irrevocable and everlasting.

Then, unbelievably, at 32, Stacey learned *she* had colon cancer, Stage II. She dodged that bullet, though, and survived to marry her sweetheart, Mike. It was a splendid day, a celebration of life renewed. To Francie, as flower girl, they gave a talking teddy bear; their recorded voices thanked her. At the end, Stacey added: "Remember, I love you up to the sky."

Soon, Stacey was in the midst of a new struggle, to have or to adopt a child. Finally, the agency that helped me find Francie found beautiful Gabriella for Stacey and Mike. The hard times seemed banished for good.

Last December 23, although feeling ill, Stacey was determined to bring 19-month-old Gabi to my house for a holiday visit. Instead, Stacey landed in intensive care with streptococcal pneumonia. Sedated, on IV antibiotics, her body fought to heal.

It was no one's fault, but the next night, Stacey just stopped breathing. By the time she was stable, a brain scan showed almost no cortical activity. Despite prayers that stormed heaven, she never wakened. I remember the call from Stacey's sister. I put down the phone and wept, "I'll never hear her voice again!" Months have passed. Stacey is still on a respirator and feeding tube, but she will never recover.

Recently, the kids and I were culling their toys for a charity. Gently tucked in a closet corner, we found "wedding bear." We tidied it up and gave it a new satin hair band. The recorder box was dangling. Would it work? We installed new batteries. And that irreplaceable voice said, "Hi Francie! This is Aunt Stacey!"

Those few words brought us such solace. Stacey's voice on tape sent a reminder that her love for us was irrevocable and everlasting. As she said, she loved us "up to the sky."

There may be many kinds of immortality. This one I know for sure: Stacey's voice telling me that no one who truly loves and is loved in return is lost to us.

The Trip of Her Life

BY
Linda
Stasi

I knew I had to do something to help. And it needed to be more than packing up relief supplies. I'd tried that, but it didn't assuage the helplessness I felt after Hurricane Katrina ripped away a chunk of our country and with it so many lives.

I never imagined, though, that "doing something" would mean driving a tractor trailer 1,450 miles to stricken Gulfport, Mississippi—or that this trip into hell would bring me the greatest blessing of my life.

A week after Katrina struck, I went to a site where donations were being collected—and ended up volunteering to drive in a 17-truck convoy organized and paid for by a New York businessman. Our goal: to transport 100 tons of supplies to hurricane victims.

The morning we left, I was terrified. Drive a tractor trailer? Me? My friend Connie Simmons, a lawyer and television producer, was coming along, and we both assumed that the other drivers—mostly men—were professional truckers who'd laugh us off the road. We couldn't have been more wrong.

Our group included a flight attendant, a former marine, a Wall Street whiz kid, a postal worker, a retired cop who'd brought along her six-year-old daughter, and a firefighter from the first New York City firehouse to lose a man on 9/11. Not to mention our leader, Hector Hoyos, CEO of the Hoyos Group, a technology consultancy firm. In other words, Americans from all kinds of backgrounds who might never have met if it hadn't been for this mission.

> The morning we left, I was terrified. Drive a tractor trailer? Me?

People started yelling "God Bless" and "You go, girls!" as I pulled out in my rig (after driving more than 1,000 miles, I get to say "my rig"). And then the fear turned to excitement. Whenever a truck broke down, all 17 of our driving teams pulled over and waited for repairs. If you've never stood by the highway while 18-wheelers speed by close enough to shave a mustache, consider yourself unfortunate. You meet the nicest people that way.

Driving south, we slept in our trucks and ate at truck stops. At one café, I watched the former cop and her daughter bow their heads, say grace, and eat their grilled

The author, at the wheel, with Connie Simmons

cheese sandwiches. Sitting down to join them, I felt blessed. With so much talk of economic and racial divides in the wake of Katrina, our group was proof that disaster can breed unity—and that the worst of times can bring out the best in us.

Kindness on Credit

BY
Andrea
Atkins

A few weeks after my father died, my friend Barbara invited me to lunch, to comfort me and lift my spirits. We had met when our daughters were in nursery school together, and she'd known my dad, Norman Atkins, a professional singer with a beautiful, deep baritone. At age 30, my father made a successful concert debut at Carnegie Hall, and over the years, his career flourished—he sang with the New York City Opera and performed solo with every major U.S. symphony orchestra, as well as on Broadway, TV, radio, and in theaters across the country.

But at the time of his debut, my father had very little money and a wife and young son to support. Back then, my parents lived in Washington Heights, in New York City. To his rescue came the neighborhood butcher, Sig Lowenthal, a German immigrant and a friend of my grandmother's. He offered my parents credit.

This became family legend—how for a whole year, Mom and Dad never laid out a dime for meat. My mother told this story often, gratitude for Mr. Lowenthal's generosity still in her voice. "And then," she'd add, "we paid back every cent."

Maybe good people are meant to come together— and to take care of one another.

By the time I was born, my parents had moved to the suburbs. But as I grew up, I heard about Sig the benevolent butcher. And from time to time, my mother would take me to the city, where we would visit him. I still remember that shop, with its sawdust-covered floor. While the grown-ups chatted, I would eat a slice of bologna and push the sawdust into piles, pretending they were sand castles.

Now, as Barbara and I sat over lunch, we began to talk about our families. I told her how much I regretted that my children would not have their grandfather in their lives. She sympathized, reminiscing about how much her grandfather had meant to her.

"What did he do for a living?" I asked.

"He was a butcher," she replied.

I knew that Barbara's maiden name was Lowenthal. Suddenly, something clicked.

"Your grandfather was Sig Lowenthal?"

The generous butcher, Sig Lowenthal, 1955

"Yes," she said, shocked that I knew. Tears immediately burned in my eyes. I was practically speechless, though I finally managed to explain. And then I felt a pang. My father had met Barbara many times, and surely he would have wanted to tell her himself what her grandfather's kindness had meant to him.

Yet I can't help but feel that discovering the connection is a real blessing. When I see my daughter Sophie playing with Barbara's daughter, Hailey, I think that maybe there is a plan in this sometimes chaotic world. Maybe good people are meant to come together—and to take care of one another. And maybe, just maybe, we're all connected in a way we can't even see.

About the Contributors

Elmaz Abinader is writer, activist, and professor. She has written *Children of the Roojme, a Family's Journey from Lebanon, and In the Country of my Dreams.* She lives in Oakland, California, with her husband.

Andrea Atkins writes magazine articles for national women's magazines, and teaches writing workshops. She lives in Rye, New York, with her husband and two children.

Rachel Balducci is a wife, mom, writer, and a newspaper columnist. She blogs about raising five boys at testosterhome.blogspot.com and lives in Augusta, Georgia, with her family.

Jan Barker is a writer and mother of two. She is currently at work on a memoir and lives in New York City.

Elizabeth Berg is the author of eighteen novels, two works of nonfiction, and two collections of short stories. She has two daughters, two grandchildren and one dog.

Maeve Binchy is an Irish novelist and newspaper columnist who has written fifteen novels, five collections of short stories, one work of non-fiction, one novella and one play. She lives in Dalkey, Ireland, with her husband.

Sarah Bird is the author of seven novels, the latest being *How Perfect Is That.* She lives in Austin, Texas, with her husband and their son.

Betsy Carter is the author of the bestselling memoir, *Nothing to Fall Back On.* She has also written two novels, the latest of which is *Swim to Me.* Currently, she writes for several national magazines. She lives in New York City.

Chris Chesak joined the Idaho National Guard in 2003 and wrote for *The Idaho Statesman.* In civilian life, he works as a nonprofit consultant, grant writer and fund-raiser. He lives in Boise, Idaho, with his wife and two daughters.

Leah Hager Cohen is the author of four non-fiction books and three novels. She writes about her mom's continuing journey at leahhagercohen.com and lives near Boston, Massachusetts.

Claire Cook is the author of five books, including *Must Love Dogs* and, most recently, *Summer Blowout*. Her next novel, *The Wildwater Walking Club* will be released in May 2009. She lives in Scituate, Massachusetts, with her husband.

Kelly Corrigan is the author of *The Middle Place* and the creator of circusofcancer.org, a website for friends of women with breast cancer. She blogs at kellycorrigan.com and lives in California with her husband and two daughters.

Melinda Santa Cruz lives with her husband and daughter in Escondido, California.

Chitra Banerjee Divakaruni is an award-winning author and poet. She has written fourteen books and currently teaches at the University of Houston. She lives in Houston, Texas, with her husband and two sons.

Firoozeh Dumas is the bestselling author of *Funny in Farsi: A Memoir of Growing Up Iranian in America* and *Laughing Without an Accent.* She lives with her husband and two children in northern California.

Lucinda Franks is the author of *My Father's Secret War,* as well as *Waiting Out A War,* and *Wild Apples.* She won a Pulitzer Prize for her reporting at the *New York Times.* She lives in New York City with her husband and two children.

Cecile Gilmer's work has been published in the *Los Angeles Times,* and broadcast on NPR. She is currently working on a memoir and lives in Utah with her husband, their two dogs, and four cats.

Alice Hoffman is the author of twenty-one novels, two books of short fiction, and eight books for children and young adults. Her most recent book is *The Story Sisters.* She currently lives in Boston and New York.

Ann Hood is the author of eight novels, one memoir, a non-fiction book on writing and a collection of short stories. Her work has appeared in numerous magazines. She lives in Rhode Island with her husband and their children.

Kate Jacobs is the *New York Times* bestselling author of *Comfort Food*, *The Friday Night Knitting Club*, *Knit Two*, and, most recently, *Knit the Season*. She lives in Southern California with her husband and their dog, Baxter.

Mike Leonard has been a reporter for *Today* on NBC for 28 years. He is the author *The Ride of Our Lives: Roadside Lessons of an American Family*. Leonard has four grown children and three grandchildren, and resides in Winnetka, Illinois, with his wife.

Elinor Lipman is the author of nine novels, one of which has been made into a feature film, and a collection of short stories. Her essays can be read at elinorlipman.com. She splits her time between New York City and Massachusetts.

Cammie McGovern is the author of *The Art of Seeing* and *Eye Contact*. She is one of the founders of Whole Children, and lives in Amherst, Massachusetts, with her husband and three children.

Jacquelyn Mitchard is the bestselling author of twelve novels and three children's books. Her latest novel is *Look Both Ways*. She is the mother of seven and lives south of Madison, Wisconsin.

Molly O'Neill was the food columnist for the *New York Times Magazine* and the host of the PBS series *Great Food*. She is the author of three cookbooks and *Mostly True: A Memoir of Family, Food, and Baseball.* She lives in New York City.

Jodi Picoult is the bestselling author of sixteen novels, three of which were made into television movies and one of which is a feature film. She has won numerous awards and accolades for her writing. She and her husband live in Hanover, New Hampshire, with their three children.

Jessica Queller is the author of *Pretty Is What Changes: Impossible Choices, the Breast Cancer Gene, and How I Defied My Destiny.* She works as a television writer in Los Angeles.

Luanne Rice is the *New York Times* bestselling author of more than twenty-one novels. Her latest work is a collaboration entitled *The Geometry of Sisters.* Rice resides in New York City and on the Connecticut shoreline.

Cathleen Schine is the author of seven novels, most recently *The New Yorkers.* She has written articles for numerous magazines, including *The New Yorker* and the *New York Times Book Review.* She lives in New York City.

Liz Smith is a New York gossip columnist. She is the author of the bestselling memoir, *Natural Blonde,* and *Dishing: Great Dish—And Dishes—From America's Most Beloved Gossip Columnist.* She lives in New York City.

Linda Stasi is a writer for the *New York Post.* She is the author of *Looking Good is the Best Revenge, Boomer Babes, A Field Guide to Impossible Men,* and *Simply Beautiful.* She lives in New York City.

Sascha Zuger is a travel novelist, freelance writer, and public radio commentator. She is the author of *Dancing Underwater,* a memoir, and *Girl Overboard,* a novel under the pen name Aimee Ferris. She lives in New York with her son.

Index

Photo Credits

All personal imagery: Courtesy of Authors

ThinkStock/Jupiter Images: 2

iStockphoto: 6, 10, 28, 40, 66, 76, 98, 102, 106, 124, 128

Workbook Stock/Jupiter Images: 14

Rita Maas/Botanica/Jupiter Images: 18

Image Source/Jupiter Images: 22

Dolding/Age Fotostock: 32

Karin Smeds/Gorilla Creative Images/Getty Images: 36

Elizabeth Simpson/Photographer's Choice/Getty Images: 44

Dennis Hallinan/Jupiter Images: 50

Charles Gullung/Photonica/Getty Images: 54

Botanica/Jupiter Images: 58

First Light/Gemstone Images/Getty Images: 62

Inside/Jupiter Images: 72

Gazimal/Iconica/Getty Images: 80

Photononstop/Jupiter Images: 84

Martin Lof/ANYONE/Getty Images: 88

StockFood Creative/Getty Images: 92

Jen Munkvold/FoodPix/Jupiter Images: 110

Image Source Black/Getty Images: 114

The Image Bank/Getty Images: 120

Nick White/Digital Vision/Getty Images: 132

Roam Images/Jupiter Images: 136

Louise Lister/Getty Images: 140

Copyright © 2009 by Hearst Communications, Inc.

Library of Congress Cataloging-in-Publication Data

Blessings : reflections on gratitude, love, and what makes us happy /
from the Editors of Good Housekeeping.
     p. cm.
  Includes index.
  ISBN 978-1-58816-780-4
  1. Gratitude. I. Good Housekeeping Institute (New York, N.Y.)
  BF575.G68B56 2009
  814'.6080353--dc22

                        2008054484

10 9 8 7 6 5 4 3 2 1

Published by Hearst Books
A division of Sterling Publishing Co., Inc.
387 Park Avenue South, New York, NY 10016

Good Housekeeping and Hearst Books are trademarks
of Hearst Communications, Inc.

www.goodhousekeeping.com

For information about custom editions, special sales, premium and corporate
purchases, please contact Sterling Special Sales Department at 800-805-5489
or specialsales@sterlingpublishing.com.

Distributed in Canada by Sterling Publishing
c/o Canadian Manda Group, 165 Dufferin Street
Toronto, Ontario, Canada M6K 3H6

Distributed in Australia by Capricorn Link (Australia) Pty. Ltd.
P.O. Box 704, Windsor, NSW 2756 Australia

Manufactured in China

Sterling ISBN 978-1-58816-780-4

SPECIAL BONUS!
Redeem Today!

12 ISSUE SUBSCRIPTION

Included in your book purchase is a one year subscription to Good Housekeeping ($5 value). Activate your subscription NOW! Just fill out the information below, cut out this form and mail to:

Good Housekeeping PO Box 7529, Red Oak, IA 51591-0529

Please include original receipt. One request per purchase. Offer expires September 30, 2010.

Name   *(please print)*

Address

City/State/Zip

Email Address
If you do not wish to receive your subscription, please see back for refund details.

REDEEM TODAY!
One year of Good Housekeeping

SUBSCRIPTION CHECKLIST

☐ *Fill out subscription card*

☐ *Include original receipt*

☐ *Mail back to Good Housekeeping*